FORBIDDEN TOPICS

Forbidden Topics

Did I say that Out Loud?

JOEL HAWKSLEY

J & Washington Network

Dedication

This book is dedicated to everyone who's ever realized, "We Can't Make This Shit Up."

We navigate a world where politics define us, yet we tiptoe around them to avoid offense. Religion, a pillar meant to be shared to save the world, is often kept close to the vest, lest we be judged or judge others. Wealth, whether flaunted or hidden and need, whether met or unmet, sit uncomfortably in our conversations. And then there's that deep desire—driven by our instincts to reproduce or simply to stimulate our exotic cravings—veiled in secrecy, even as we seek companionship without daring to discuss the unspoken expectations of intimacy.

In this collection of satirical poetry, I aim to shine a light on the vices, follies, and contradictions that permeate our society. Through irony, wit, humor, and ridicule, these poems critique the pillars of politics, religion, money, and sex— subjects that, though often shrouded in taboo, define much of the human experience.

May these words inspire reflection, laughter, and perhaps a bit of discomfort as we confront the truths we often leave unspoken.

INTRODUCTION

Greetings, dear reader. Welcome to a journey through the vivid, absurd, and often unsettling world of "Forbidden Topics." In this collection of satirical poetry, The aim is to shine a light on the vices, follies, and contradictions that permeate our society. Through irony, wit, humor, and ridicule, these poems critique the pillars of politics, religion, money, and sex —subjects that, though often shrouded in taboo, define much of the human experience.

CONTENTS

PART II
RELIGION

PART III

MONEY

Contents

PREFACE

Satirical poetry has long been a powerful tool for social commentary. From the sharp-tongued verses of Juvenal in ancient Rome to the biting wit of Jonathan Swift and the clever wordplay of Dorothy Parker, satire has been used to expose the hypocrisy and absurdity of those in power and to question societal norms. It is through satire that poets can address uncomfortable truths, challenge the status quo, and provoke thought and discussion.

In "Forbidden Topics," I explore the contemporary landscape of politics, religion, money, and sex. These themes are not chosen lightly. They are the cornerstones of our lives, the forces that shape our world and influence our behavior. Yet, they are often treated as untouchable, too sacred or too profane to be openly examined. This book seeks to break those barriers, to peel back the layers of decorum and delve into the heart of these subjects with a critical, and often humorous, eye.

Introduction to Satirical Poetry and Its Role in Social Commentary

Satirical poetry, at its core, is a mirror held up to society, reflecting its virtues and vices in exaggerated and often comical ways. It uses humor not merely to entertain but to reveal truths that might be too uncomfortable to confront directly. By highlighting the absurdities and contradictions in our actions and beliefs, satire prompts us to question, to rethink, and, hopefully, to change.

In today's world, where information flows at an unprecedented speed and public figures are constantly under scrutiny, satire remains as relevant as ever. It cuts through the noise, offering clarity through exaggeration and humor. In an era of political spin, religious dogma, financial greed, and sexual exploitation, satirical poetry provides a necessary counterbalance, a voice that dares to speak out against the pretense and the folly.

Explanation of the Themes Covered in the Book

Politics: The realm of power, where leaders are often more concerned with maintaining their positions than with serving the people. This section explores the theater of elections, the hypocrisy of political promises, and the corruption that lurks behind closed doors. It is a reflection on the absurdities of governance and the often farcical nature of political discourse.

Religion: A domain of deep belief and spiritual seeking, yet also one of dogma, hypocrisy, and exploitation. Here, we delve into the contradictions of faith, the commercialization of spirituality, and the moral failures of religious leaders. It is a critique of how religion, meant to uplift, can sometimes be used to manipulate and control.

Money: The lifeblood of modern society, a source of both opportunity and oppression. This section examines the greed that drives economic systems, the disparities between rich and poor, and the ethical compromises made in the pursuit of wealth. It is an exploration of how money shapes our lives and our values.

Sex: The most intimate of human experiences, yet one fraught with social and moral complexities. In these poems, we confront the taboos surrounding sexuality, the commodification of desire, and the power dynamics inherent in sexual relationships. It is a candid look at the interplay of love, lust, and societal expectations.

Through these themes, "Forbidden Topics" aims to provoke, to amuse, and to enlighten. It is my hope that as you read these poems, you will find not only humor but also a deeper understanding of the world around you. Satire, after all, is not just about laughter—it is about seeing the truth through the lens of wit and irony. So, let us embark on this journey together, with open minds and a willingness to confront the uncomfortable. For it is in the forbidden that we often find the most profound insights.

PART I

POLITICS

This part of the book provides a satirical examination of politics, highlighting the absurdities, contradictions, and vices within the political landscape.

| 1 |

The Puppet Show

In halls of power, strings unseen,
Marionettes on stages preen.
Behind the curtain, shadows pull,
The leaders dance, their voices dull.

| 2 |

Election Circus

Step right up, see the grand parade,
Candidates in costumes made.
Promises are flying high,
Underneath, the truth, a lie.

| 3 |

Promises, Promises

A vow today, forgotten soon,
A politician's favorite tune.
They speak of change, but stay the same,
In this deceitful, endless game.

| 4 |

Red vs. Blue

Two sides, one coin, they clash and fight,
A spectacle both day and night.
Divide the people, gain the power,
In unity, their influence would cower.

| 5 |

The Lobbyist's Lament

In smoky rooms, they trade their gold,
For influence, a story old.
Policies are bought and sold,
As truth and justice, left out in the cold.

| 6 |

Scandal Season

Each year brings a fresh disgrace,
A politician's fall from grace.
But scandals pass, the memory fades,
New lies, new faces, same charades.

| 7 |

The Emperor's New Policy

Behold the leader's latest plan,
Invisible to the common man.
With grandeur, it is hailed as grand,
But substance slips right through the hand.

| 8 |

The Spin Doctor

Twist the truth, reshape the tale,
Turn a storm into a gale.
In media's hands, the narrative bends,
Truth distorted, as it descends.

| 9 |

Gerrymander Game

Lines are drawn in twisted ways,
To keep the power, to extend the stays.
Voters corralled in clusters tight,
Fair representation, out of sight.

| 10 |

The Politician's Mask

A smile wide, a heart so cold,
A mask of warmth, ambitions bold.
Behind the charm, a ruthless mind,
Seeking gain, the rest behind.

| 11 |

Filibuster Follies

With endless talk, they stall the vote,
On a sea of words, the bills do float.
A tactic old, to halt and slow,
Progress hampered, as they blow.

| 12 |

Campaign Trail of Tears

Through towns and cities, they do roam,
Seeking votes far from their home.
They promise much, deliver less,
Leaving hopes in disarray, a mess.

| 13 |

Senate Shenanigans

In chambers grand, the games they play,
Decisions made in disarray.
Debates as endless as the night,
The public waits, devoid of sight.

| 14 |

The Debate Debacle

Two podiums, a battle staged,
Words as weapons, the war is waged.
No answers found, just points to score,
In this rhetorical uproar.

| 15 |

Political Pantomime

A scripted show, each move precise,
Emotions feigned, intentions nice.
But underneath the actor's guise,
Lies the truth they seek to disguise.

| **16** |

The Policy Pendulum

Swinging left, then swinging right,
Policies change with every fight.
Progress stifled in the sway,
Caught between the night and day.

| 17 |

Party Line Pratfalls

Loyalty to the party line,
Blinds them to the truth's own shine.
In echo chambers, they do shout,
Ideas stagnant, no fresh out.

| **18** |

Earmark Escapades

Hidden within the budget's lines,
Special favors, secret signs.
For constituents, a special treat,
While others' needs go incomplete.

| 19 |

The Bureaucratic Maze

Endless forms and red tape walls,
In the maze, ambition stalls.
Decisions lost in endless files,
While progress waits in endless piles.

| **20** |

Diplomatic Disasters

With handshakes warm and smiles fake,
Deals are made, for power's sake.
But promises in ink are thin,
As nations doubt what lies within.

| 21 |

The Corruption Carousel

Round and round the scandals spin,
From boardroom plots to political sin.
Each time the carousel does go,
A new face, but the same old show.

| **22** |

The Election Aftermath

Victory cheers turn to policy fears,
As promises fade, reality nears.
The public waits with bated breath,
For hope reborn or hope's own death.

| 23 |

Backroom Deals

In secret rooms, behind closed doors,
The deals are made, the spirit soars.
But what was gained and what was lost,
In democracy, we bear the cost.

| **24** |

The Populist Parade

A leader rises, speaks the crowd,
With promises, they cheer so loud.
But substance lacks behind the praise,
As dreams dissolve in future haze.

| 25 |

The Lobbyists' Ball

In grand ballrooms, the lobbyists sway,
To the tune of influence, they play.
Politicians join the dance,
In this corrupt, entangled trance.

PART II

RELIGION

This section of the book explores the intricate and often contradictory nature of religion, using satire to reveal the absurdities and hypocrisies within spiritual institutions and beliefs.

| 26 |

Heaven's Gatekeepers

At heaven's gates, they guard the way,
Deciding who can pass or stay.
With judgments harsh, they rule supreme,
A distant echo of a dream.

| 27 |

Faith for Sale

In temples grand, the wares are sold,
Faith packaged neat in shapes of gold.
For those who pay, salvation's near,
A price to cleanse the soul from fear.

| 28 |

Preacher's Gold

A preacher stands with gilded grace,
Riches hidden, truth displaced.
With every sermon, wealth they gain,
While followers in hope remain.

| 29 |

Holy Wars

Under banners bright, the armies march,
For sacred cause, their throats do parch.
In holy wars, the blood is spilled,
By faith's command, the fields are tilled.

| 30 |

Miracle Merchants

Selling wonders, miracles fake,
In desperate hope, believers take.
The merchants laugh behind the scenes,
As pockets swell with ill-gained means.

| 31 |

Divine Irony

In holy texts, the ironies shine,
A loving God, with wrath divine.
Commands of peace, yet wars ordained,
In faith's own name, destruction rained.

| **32** |

Sins and Virtues

The line between the sin and grace,
Shifts with time and culture's face.
What once was wrong is now just fine,
And virtues fall with each new sign.

| 33 |

The Pious Politician

In public eye, they kneel and pray,
But in the dark, their morals sway.
The pious front, a mask so thin,
Concealing greed and hidden sin.

| **34** |

Prosperity Gospel

Blessings bought with every cent,
The poor are told their cash is lent.
In faith's own bank, their wealth will grow,
But only preachers see the flow.

| 35 |

Sacred Scandals

Behind the altar, secrets kept,
Of whispered sins, where angels wept.
The sacred trust in shadows falls,
As scandals breach the holy walls.

| 36 |

The Sermon's Script

Each Sunday brings a scripted tale,
To keep the flock within the pale.
With passion feigned, the words resound,
But meaning lost in echoes drowned.

| 37 |

Confessional Confusion

Kneeling down to confess the sins,
The penance given, the shame begins.
But are they cleansed, or just deceived,
In rituals that faith believed?

| **38** |

The Cult of Personality

In leaders' names, they place their trust,
To follow blind, obey they must.
A cult of personality,
Where faith's replaced with vanity.

| 39 |

Religious Rivalries

Each faith proclaims it holds the key,
To truth and heaven's mystery.
But rival gods and prophets rise,
And leave the faithful polarized.

| **40** |

Saints and Sinners

Saints held high, sinners cast low,
But who decides the status quo?
For saints have sinned, and sinners pray,
In faith's own court, the gray holds sway.

| 41 |

The Holy Hypocrite

A righteous face, a heart of stone,
In sacred halls, their sins are sown.
The holy hypocrite maintains,
A life of lies beneath the chains.

| 42 |

Doctrinal Disputes

The doctrines shift, the schisms grow,
Each sect believes it best to know.
The truth is lost in endless fights,
As dogma blinds their inner sights.

| 43 |

The Believer's Burden

To follow faith, a burdened path,
With doubts and fears, and holy wrath.
The believer's burden, heavy borne,
In search of light, through night and morn.

| 44 |

Pulpit Puppeteers

From pulpit high, they pull the strings,
Controlling thoughts, dictating things.
The puppeteers in robes so grand,
Manipulate with steady hand.

| **45** |

Faith Healing Fables

With hands outstretched, they claim to cure,
But healing's price is never pure.
For those who trust in fables told,
Find sickness stays, while hope grows cold.

| 46 |

The Prayer Pyramid

Prayers ascend in pyramid scheme,
With hopes and dreams, a faithful stream.
But those at top reap all the grace,
While others linger in their place.

| 47 |

The Conversion Conundrum

To save the souls, they seek to turn,
In faith's own fires, converts burn.
But forced beliefs, a hollow win,
In hearts unchanged, the doubts begin.

| **48** |

Religious Reformations

The calls for change in sacred rites,
Bring clashes, wars, and endless fights.
Each reformation, hope reborn,
Yet leaves the faithful torn and worn.

| **49** |

The Divine Dictator

A deity with iron will,
Commands the faithful to fulfill.
The divine dictator's harsh decree,
Leaves little room for liberty.

| 50 |

Afterlife Allegories

In tales of heaven and of hell,
The faithful find their fears do swell.
For what awaits beyond this life,
Is shrouded deep in myth and strife.

PART III

MONEY

This section uses satire to critique various aspects of the modern economic system, exposing the greed, corruption, and inequities that permeate the world of money.

| **51** |

The Golden Calf

In modern times, the calf is gold,
Worshiped more than stories old.
Its altars rise in banks and malls,
Where greed and wealth erect their halls.

| 52 |

The Rat Race

In endless chase, they seek the prize,
With weary feet and blinded eyes.
The rat race winds through days and nights,
With happiness just out of sight.

| 53 |

Credit Card Confessions

Plastic promises of instant gain,
Lead to chains of endless pain.
Confessions made at billing time,
In debts accrued through heedless crime.

| 54 |

The Rich Man's Plight

With riches vast, they lie awake,
Fearing thieves that wealth could take.
The rich man's plight, a life of dread,
Guarding gold beneath the bed.

| 55 |

The Taxman's Tale

The taxman cometh, hand held out,
With complex forms, and claims of doubt.
In labyrinths of rules they dwell,
Extracting wealth in bureaucratic hell.

| 56 |

Fortune's Fool

One day rich, the next day poor,
Fortune's fool knows neither shore.
In wealth's embrace or poverty's clutch,
Their life's dictated by fickle luck.

| 57 |

Billionaire's Burden

With yachts and jets, they seem so free,
Yet burdened by their own ennui.
For wealth can't buy the things that last,
Love and joy, both long since past.

| **58** |

The Stock Market Circus

In trading pits, the gamblers play,
A circus act of gains and sway.
The market's rise, the market's fall,
A frenzied dance that grips them all.

| 59 |

The Hedge Fund Hustle

Behind closed doors, the deals are made,
In shadowed rooms where fortunes trade.
The hedge fund hustle, quick and sly,
To win the game while others cry.

| **60** |

The CEO's Bonus

With profits high, the workers wait,
For crumbs that fall from CEO's plate.
A bonus big for corporate kings,
While layoffs cut the common strings.

| 61 |

The Ponzi Scheme

With promises of easy gain,
They build a house on fragile frame.
The Ponzi scheme grows tall and wide,
Until it crashes, and truths collide.

| 62 |

Wall Street Wolves

In tailored suits, the wolves they roam,
Through Wall Street's halls, their hunting home.
With sharpest teeth and cunning eyes,
They feast on those who trust their lies.

| **63** |

The Banker's Bailout

When banks do fall, the public pays,
To save the few from their own ways.
The banker's bailout, unjust, absurd,
Rewards the reckless, unearned.

| **64** |

The Speculator's Spin

In markets vast, they place their bets,
With little care for long-term debts.
The speculator's spin is wild,
A risky game, both cruel and mild.

| 65 |

The Greed Gospel

In sermons loud, they praise the gold,
A gospel new, both bright and bold.
The greed gospel spreads its creed,
To worship wealth, ignore the need.

| **66** |

The Debt Disaster

In credit traps, they find despair,
With rising debts they can't repair.
A disaster born of loans and greed,
Leaves families broken, hearts that bleed.

| 67 |

The Mortgage Meltdown

In dreams of homes, they find their chains,
As mortgage rates bring endless pains.
The meltdown hits, the values fall,
Leaving debts that drown them all.

| **68** |

Capitalist Carnage

In factories closed and towns decayed,
The cost of wealth is fully paid.
The capitalist carnage leaves,
A trail of loss that few perceive.

| 69 |

The Wealth Gap Whimsy

The rich grow richer, poor remain,
In wealth gap's whimsy, few complain.
For dreams of climbing, hopes so high,
Keep them chasing, till they die.

| 70 |

The Pension Predicament

In golden years, they seek respite,
But pensions fail, a bitter bite.
The predicament leaves them bare,
After decades of work and care.

| 71 |

The Investor's Illusion

In stocks they trust, their future bright,
But illusions crumble overnight.
Investors wake to shattered dreams,
In a market's fickle, endless schemes.

| 72 |

The Economic Exodus

As jobs move out, the towns decay,
In economic exodus, they pray.
For better times and stable ground,
In empty streets, no hope is found.

| **73** |

The Corporate Conundrum

Big business grows, small ventures die,
A conundrum vast beneath the sky.
For corporate power reigns supreme,
In every sector, every dream.

| 74 |

The Consumer's Curse

They buy and buy, yet never fill,
The void within, the endless will.
The consumer's curse, a cycle spins,
Of wants and needs, where no one wins.

| 75 |

The Profiteer's Plight

In profit's chase, they lose their soul,
A plight unseen, a costly toll.
For money's gain brings empty heart,
And tears their very self apart.

PART IV

SEX

This section delves into the complexities of human sexuality, relationships, and desires, using satire to expose the ironies, hypocrisies, and absurdities within these intimate aspects of life.

| 76 |

Bedroom Politics

In chambers dim, the power plays,
Where whispers sway and love betrays.
In bedroom's realm, the games are fierce,
As secrets shared, the hearts they pierce.

| **77** |

The Dating Game

Swipe left, swipe right, the endless scroll,
In search of love, a fractured goal.
The dating game, a modern plight,
With shallow hearts and fleeting light.

| **78** |

Love for Sale

In alleys dark and streets aglow,
Love's sold for prices, high and low.
Transactions cold, desires bought,
In places where the heart is naught.

| 79 |

The Purity Myth

They preach of purity's bright glow,
Yet hide the truth they dare not show.
For human hearts, with passion burn,
And purity's myth, they soon unlearn.

| 80 |

Taboo Tango

In shadows deep, the dances start,
Forbidden steps of aching heart.
The taboo tango, secret dance,
Of hidden love and furtive glance.

| 81 |

Desire's Dilemma

Desire burns with fierce intent,
Yet leaves the soul in discontent.
A tangled web of want and need,
Where hearts and minds in conflict bleed.

| **82** |

The Seduction of Power

With power's touch, they feel the lure,
A seduction sweet, yet never pure.
In beds of might, the deals are made,
As virtue fades, in power's shade.

| **83** |

Intimacy Ironies

In moments close, they feel the strain,
Of intimacy's tender pain.
The ironies of hearts laid bare,
In love's own game, where all is fair.

| 84 |

The Romantic Ruse

With roses red and words so sweet,
They weave a ruse where hearts do meet.
But underneath the charming guise,
Lies emptiness, and well-told lies.

| 85 |

The Affair's Aftermath

In secret trysts, they find delight,
Yet pay the price in darkened night.
The aftermath of passion's fire,
Leaves ashes cold, and hearts in mire.

| **86** |

Sexual Stereotypes

They paint the genders in bold hues,
With stereotypes that they refuse.
To see beyond the narrow frames,
And understand the human flames.

| **87** |

The Passion Play

On stages set, they act the part,
With scripted lines that break the heart.
The passion play of love's charade,
In acts performed, where truths do fade.

Erotic Expectations

With fantasies that seldom match,
Reality, a different batch.
The expectations, high and wild,
Leave hearts and bodies oft beguiled.

| 89 |

The Temptation Trap

Temptation whispers in the ear,
With promises both sweet and clear.
Yet in its grip, they find the snare,
That traps the soul in deep despair.

| 90 |

Lust and Lies

In lust's embrace, they find deceit,
With lies that make the heart's pulse beat.
The truths obscured by passion's flame,
Leave love and trust in sullied name.

| **91** |

The Fantasy Facade

Behind closed doors, the fantasies rise,
With facades that bring the sweet disguise.
In dreams fulfilled, yet hearts still yearn,
For deeper bonds that they discern.

| 92 |

Forbidden Flings

In secret places, hearts entwine,
With flings forbidden, they align.
The thrill of what they should not taste,
In hidden moments, gone to waste.

| 93 |

The Carnal Carnival

In carnival of flesh and sin,
They lose themselves in lust's own din.
The carnal pleasures, wild and free,
Leave shadows where the light should be.

| 94 |

The Affair's Allure

The forbidden fruit, so sweet and ripe,
Calls to those who dare to swipe.
The allure of an affair, so strong,
Yet leaves a trail of right and wrong.

| 95 |

The Bedroom Bargain

In beds they strike the silent deals,
With touch and whisper, power feels.
The bargains made in darkness deep,
Are secrets that they swore to keep.

| 96 |

The Infidelity Folly

In moments weak, they stray from path,
In infidelity's cruel wrath.
The folly known, yet still pursued,
Leaves lives and loves in darkness hewed.

| **97** |

The Seducer's Scheme

With charm and wit, they set the trap,
A scheme so sly, a gentle tap.
To lure the heart with false pretense,
And leave it broken, in defense.

| 98 |

The Sexual Spectrum

In colors bright, the spectrum shines,
With varied loves and diverse lines.
Yet judgment falls on those who stray,
From norms that narrow minds portray.

| 99 |

The Love Triangle

In three's a crowd, the tensions rise,
With jealous hearts and secret lies.
The love triangle's tangled web,
Leaves all involved in sorrow's ebb.

| **100** |

The Intimacy Illusion

In closeness sought, they find the rift,
An illusion grand, a fleeting gift.
For intimacy's promise bright,
Can fade like shadows in the night.